Defending American Values

By

Robert Villegas

Defending American Values
By
Robert Villegas

Copyright 2020 by Robert Villegas

Email: robertv1989@outlook.com

www.robertvillegas.com

Twitter: @robertvillega18

ISBN: 9781660374168
Imprint: Independently published

www.documentservicesinternational.com

Dedicated to our Troops

3

Table of Contents

The American Spirit

I have been thinking a lot about the American spirit lately and it has caused me to explore and appreciate literature about life during the 19th Century. There are many movies, novels and history books that depict pioneer days and the values of people who lived during that time and many of them do a pretty good job of capturing the spirit that built our nation and made it strong. Here is what I have gathered so far:

-Almost the entire 19th century was a time of positive expectations with a growing sense of optimism. It was a time of hope, trust and benevolence. These were not blind Pollyannaish hopes but the result of a conviction that man could improve his life and surroundings through hard work and independent thinking. Production became an American value.

-Yet, nature is very harsh and deadly, and it took a special attitude to survive in the wilderness without the aid of modern conveniences. Men were confident in their strength and intelligence. They looked forward to building structures that would protect them against the elements, and they enjoyed their lives. Pride became an American value.

-People had to make, with their own hands, many of the things they needed for survival and this made them strong and tough but also more rational since they had to be correct about what they needed. Their lives depended upon their knowledge gained through observing reality. Rational thinking became an American value.

-People were more civilized and respectful of each other because they realized that each man was a resource for knowledge and survival skills. This made them appreciate each other more and respect those among them who had shown some particular skill or ability. The good hunter or good carpenter was always prized by his contemporaries. Justice in the form of rewarding good actions became an American value.

-They could more easily tell when they were being bamboozled by someone. Their judgments had to be firmly rooted in reality and they knew that their minds must actively pursue knowledge of existence. They expected honesty and truth from others, and they learned that others valued it too. Honesty and truth became American values.

-They got angry when they felt they were being bamboozled and/or taken advantage of. Because of this, they expressed that anger and acted upon it to the point of direct violence against a thief or charlatan. Yet, most often, this violence seldom led to more than a black eye or bloody nose...the important thing was that the blackguard learned his lesson or left town. Justice in the form of punishing bad actions became an American value.

-This means they also understood that the thief and the charlatan were birds of a feather and they had no problem hating them with vigor because they understood how dangerous such people could be and how their efforts made survival, which was already hard, even harder. This was frontier justice which later became the justice system. The rule of law became an American value.

-They loved intensely and appreciated those they selected as their spouses and neighbors. Relationships were important to survival and so was self-sufficiency which strengthened friendships and shared experiences. Family and friendship became American values.

-When nature threatened, they pulled together, not out of altruism but out of self-interest. They knew that helping their neighbors through tough times helped them should they someday experience difficulties. Once the threat was over, they went back to their individual lives. Voluntary cooperation and neighborliness became American values.

-They did not make disaster into a reason for sacrifice. They got angry at the idea of sacrifice and those who would require it...even preachers (This fact has been lost beneath the emergence of self-sacrifice as it is preached in modern times). Rather, independence and self-sufficiency became American values.

-When they made a decision, they stuck with it and took responsibility for thinking and doing. So, they thought more carefully and came up with firm answers that reflected a moral perspective. Right action became an American value.

-They respected knowledge and culture and sought to bring it to the wilderness in the forms of books and theatrical presentations, music, dances and other forms of socializing. Social life and sharing knowledge became American values.

-As soon as organized society and division of labor formed, they took advantage of it but still were wary of those who would introduce paper money, debt and contract. As the saying goes, their word was their bond. Truth became an American value.

-They trusted farmers and felt they were more honest, and they distrusted merchants and people who made a living off the work of others such as speculators, bankers and lawyers. Free trade became an American value.

-They didn't like being told what to do. They preferred reason and cooperation. They resisted being forced and often carried their weapons to protect themselves. Reason, respect of others and honest discussion became American values.

-The culmination of these values was the Bill of Rights and the philosophy behind it which is individualism.

We should ask ourselves: which philosophy creates a better America? Is it the philosophy of individualism

which leads to freedom and capitalism or the philosophy
of collectivism which tells men they didn't make it?

Imagine a young man who is working hard to be a great baseball player. He is 12 years old and looks forward to a career as a professional player. He has spent hours practicing, listening to his coaches, reading books about the lives of great players such as Babe Ruth and Mickey Mantle. All of his energy is spent on learning the sport; how to run, steal bases, hit the ball and throw it accurately.

He works hard to make the All-Star Team in his local Little League and today he has hit his first home run. He is proud of his homerun and can't help his excitement and enthusiasm. On the way home from the game, he tells his father he has a good chance of making the All-Star Team. The father explodes and tells his son:

"There are a lot of good ball players who don't think they are that good. They know they didn't — look, if you've hit a home run, you didn't do it on your own. You didn't get there on your own. Your pride means nothing. You must think, 'Well, it must be because I am so good.' There are a lot of good players out there. 'It must be because I worked harder than everybody else.' Let me tell you something — there are a whole bunch of hardworking people out there.

"If you hit a home run, somebody along the way gave you some help. There was a great coach somewhere. Somebody helped create this sport for you to play. Somebody invested in ball parks and spectator stands. If you've hit a home run, you didn't do that on your own. Somebody else made that happen. "

What kind of father would say that to his son? What kind of father would destroy that young man's joy and excitement by diminishing his accomplishment? Is there any justice in that statement, any appreciation for the effort and dedication that it took that young man to be able to hit the ball that far? In the face of such an attack, would that young man be motivated to try harder in the future, knowing that at the end of the day, he will be ridiculed for his effort?

That father has killed this young man's joy and love of accomplishment. He has killed the American spirit.

Playing the Altruism Card

"Democratic 2020 hopeful Sen. Bernie Sanders on Thursday released his plan for a Green New Deal — promising that the multitrillion-dollar plan to radically overhaul the economy and combat climate change will "pay for itself" over the next 15 years.

""As president, Bernie Sanders will launch the decade of the Green New Deal, a ten-year, nationwide mobilization centered around justice and equity during which climate change will be factored into virtually every area of policy, from immigration to trade to foreign policy and beyond," his campaign said in a press release."[1]

What are Mr. Sanders' American values? From all indications, they are based upon the idea that a moral society takes care of the poor, the aged, the downtrodden, the worker, the ethnic minority, leftist intellectuals, bureaucrats, and the CEO who pays the most in campaign contributions. Like President Obama before him, his American value is sacrifice. He bemoans the fact that our constitution did not have a "re-distributive" component.

His values require that hard working people must part with their money so those who do not work hard have an equal standard of living. These "values" were stated by Karl Marx, "from each according to his ability, to each

---

[1] https://www.foxnews.com/politics/sanders-releases-16-trillion-plus-green-new-deal-plan-promises-it-will-pay-for-itself

according to his need." This is the morality that he is "doing" in his job as a politician.

How does spending 16 trillion dollars on the Green New Deal accomplish his values? And are his values really our values? Do all Americans agree that re-distribution of earnings on this massive scale will accomplish anything good? Do they think it is more important to solve our so-called energy and environmental problems with money that has yet to be earned? Do we really believe that we can make things better today by ensuring that our children and grandchildren are unable to live normal affluent lives in the future?

"In addition to promises that include reaching 100 percent renewable energy by 2030 and decarbonization by 2050 and ending unemployment by creating 20 million "good paying" jobs tied to clean energy, Sanders claims he will save families money with a host of policies -- including launching universal high-speed Internet, weatherizing homes, building new public transportation and rebuilding America's infrastructure.

"Among those promises are a $681 billion program for families and small businesses to trade in old vehicles for newer, more energy-efficient motors – a souped-up version of the Obama administration-era "Cash for Clunkers" program."[2]

Senator Sanders has just played the altruism card and the stakes of his gambit are high. In the balance is

---

[2] Ibid

whether we will continue toward bigger government and eventual collapse or make the needed changes that will get our country back on track toward freedom, individual rights and a true prosperity.

But he is correct in a sense; government spending is about morality; but not in the way he means it. The fact is that anything the government does is subject to moral evaluation; and the correct evaluation of his multi-trillion-dollar boondoggle is simply this: the Green New Deal is immoral, it is the invocation of altruism for the sake of enslaving every man, woman and child in the country.

The socialist Senator apparently does not see the connection between his ideas and the very economic circumstances in which we find ourselves. He does not realize that every borrowed dollar government spends is a dollar taken from the private economy and stimulates nothing but wasteful spending. It not only violates the individual rights of producers, it also destroys the incentive to produce more.

What is a "ten-year nationwide mobilization"? It is a deadly serious coercive imposition into the lives of every American. Under the guise of an "emergency", the government will nationalize every industry and enslave every individual in one of the most massive sacrifices of life, money and energy that the world has ever seen.

The Green New Deal is a call to action, a declaration of war and a demand that every individual dedicate his work to the state whether he benefits or not. In fact, every worker will be sacrificing for the sake of losing comfort, happiness and prosperity. Have you ever known the government to ever give back a right they have taken away? Has any massive spending program ever gotten smaller? Have they ever declared an emergency solved? Even today, they declare that our nation was at its best when we came together to fight and win a World War, or when we came together to put a man on the moon. Now they want to do it again and force us to come together to solve a problem that they can't even prove is a problem.

The Green New Deal will confiscate and spend the money now available to businesses and individuals for investment. It gives this money to government under the false assumption that government will produce better results. He calls it an investment that will pay for itself. There is no proof that the money will come back to the investor.

What Sanders does not realize is that government cannot effectively invest money *in* the private economy that originally came *from* the private economy. This merely moves money around allowing the government to rake off a big part for administrative costs (on non-productive jobs) with much of it going to boondoggles and deliberate government waste. This includes projects like cars no one will buy, energy that costs more to produce than what is already available on the free market, massive re-distributions of income that punish success. Sanders wants a revolution that creates work camps and re-education programs to make men into slaves. These endeavors will not pay for themselves. They will be taken out of the hides of people who simply want to be left alone.

A competent economist will tell you that spending does not spur production - only capital accumulation (private savings) can do that. If the myth of government spending isn't a failure of "socialist morality", then please tell me what socialist success looks like. There is no example of it in history.

What is the altruism card and how does it provide cover for socialist spending? The term "altruism card" is a metaphor for a playing card that gives the player an advantage in a card game. It invokes a privilege on the card holder that makes him temporarily immune to a loss in the particular game he is playing. In morality, the altruism card is the invocation of the morality of human sacrifice for the collective. It is the demand that government take money from the productive for the sake of a social goal of some type.

What does Senator Sanders count on when he uses the altruism card? What does he think should happen when he reminds us of our "duty" to sacrifice for others? He hopes that we will feel too guilty to stop government spending. He counts on us being too morally paralyzed to challenge the morality of sacrifice.

The altruism card has worked before and generations of teachers have been preaching sacrifice since progressives took over education; the kids are brainwashed with the notion of duty and few adults have the moral courage to say...enough. Sanders knows that all he has to do is call the Republicans cruel, heartless, evil, in the pay of corporations, unconcerned about the plight of the poor...and they'll fold like a tazed college student...every single time.

In fact, the altruism card has been used successfully by entire generations of progressive politicians. It is the tactic behind every measure that progressives have advocated since they came to prominence. It starts when they create a victim of some type and demand that charity be extended to him. Then they blame a scapegoat for the victim's suffering. They inform us that neither private charity nor the free market can take care of this victim; that private means have failed to solve the "problem"; that laissez faire ideas have, in fact, created the problem. Then they use the force of government to re-distribute money to the government (not the victim). This is forced altruism, the goal of the altruism card. This is Bernie Sanders' morality.

But the problem of the invented victim is never solved. The altruism card merely creates the pretext for exploiting the productive individual. The victim languishes in failure and poverty because the altruism card is not meant to "save" him. It is meant to enrich the collectors of sacrifice and give them a standard of living they have not earned. The victim is incidental and ignored until the next time he can be used to stoke guilt in the productive individual.

If the altruism card works today, as it does, then the progressives will try it again tomorrow...until forever. It is why the left wins politically. By their view, there can never be enough sacrificing. They will never stop demanding it. Remember, the people who pay the money never see where the money goes. They only see protestations of "doing good"; they only see the victims and trust that some type of "good" will actually be accomplished by their giving. This is what Bernie defends, a moral shell game fueled by sleight of hand with your money going into their pockets in more ways than you can imagine. This is why they come up with programs like the Green New Deal which are massive re-distribution projects controlled by them (not by Republicans). In fact, the Green New Deal is only the latest boondoggle that combines just about every leftist pipe dream into one massive slave labor camp.

For centuries we have been brainwashed about altruism as a moral virtue. But let's look at the history of some of the most common forms of altruism:

• For centuries, Kings pretended to be gods in order to justify their enslavement of citizens who were forced to give up their lives and work because it was considered good. As a representative of god, the King was able to insist that subjects give up their work and crops for the kingdom. They also had to serve in the military to support the King's wars. The result was countless battles and dead bodies, fuedalism, famine and plague, subsistence farming and ignorance.

• Governments have engaged in endless propaganda campaigns intended to convince citizens they have a duty to sacrifice for the good of the whole, whether that whole is a nation, a tribe, an ethnic group or a city. The result was the rise and fall of civilizations slowly robbed of their substance, culture and rights by thieving emperors and politicians.

• Philosophers have developed deceptive arguments intended to convince people they cannot rely on their own senses or their own minds. The goal of these schemes (such as the analytic-synthetic dichotomy) was to ensure that people sacrificed their minds, never discovered reason and believed they were too ignorant to think for themselves. The only thing men could rely on, under these schemes, was that government knew best and their only moral act was to give up their minds to "strong and powerful" leaders who forced men to sacrifice for the sake of society. Sacrifice of the mind leads to sacrifice of the body. The result was institutional plunder of countless populations of confused citizens. The result was pragmatism (realpolitik), psuedo-science and a call for "Open Societies" which were nothing more than fascist dictatorships with their attendant anti-capitalism, genocide, racism and bankruptcy.

• Progressives for over 100 years have told us that capitalism has failed, that freedom has failed, that individual rights are a myth, that the Constitution was a document of negative rights. They touted the "civilized" and "practical" nature of societies dedicated to sacrifice for the collective. They swooned over swaggering chauvinistic leaders (dictators) with the will to "make the trains run on time" and they idealized citizens enthusiastically dedicated to the "good of society". This resulted in fascism, socialism, communism and other coercive governments run by murderous brutes who started major wars and created the bloodiest century in the history of man, the century of our parents and grandparents.

So, today, when Bernie Sanders tells you that we should spend the future income of your children for the sake of his view of what is moral, he is not talking about a morality that has created any good on this earth. Throughout history, altruism has only created economic depression and hunger. It has created more plunder and murder than any other system; it is the morality of thieves, murderers, liars, gangsters and runaway politicians. It was imposed on our ancestors and today, it is being imposed on you and your posterity. You are part of the ages-old scheme of altruistic plunder. You are the target and the victim.

Senator Sanders thinks he can get away with using the altruism card. He thinks we will deny reality and follow his leadership, not to solve problems, but to adhere to the "values" that have been so beautifully sung to us all our lives. It is a haunting melody based upon a lie. All you need is love. He knows that the altruism card has been played for centuries and, with the exception of one shining moment of enlightenment, it has wrought destruction every time. He knows that if he keeps playing the music of sacrifice, he will be able to keep spending us into oblivion.

He knows that altruism is the one idea that destroys your ability to use reason. He knows it but you don't. Don't feel alone, the morality of plunder has exploited your ancestors. What makes you different? It's up to you to answer that question.

To understand why the morality card is a cynical ploy, we must ask, "what is true morality?" What makes a person good? Is it the amount of money he gives away to support Nazi concentration camps, or Johnson's Great Society or the Roman Empire or Obama's Health Care program? The answer must be "No!"

The truth is that having your earnings confiscated by government does not make you moral; it destroys your ability to *be* moral. Having your money taken from you by force makes you a victim of crime. It destroys your ability to positively affect your life because it has removed from your life the value which you could have used to improve or enjoy it.

This is why theft is immoral - it steals value - it violates rights - rights are about freedom of action - value gives you freedom of action - theft destroys your freedom of action. It doesn't matter if the theft is done by a criminal or Nancy Pelosi, you will suffer in exactly the same way regardless of who the thief might be. You lose; the criminal wins and lives to steal another day.

Morality begins with human choice, with confronting reality in order to create survival. It is about using your mind and making the right decisions about your values. It is about having the self-esteem that never feels guilty for thinking. It is about trading your best product, your skill and your time for the best products of others. It is about an ever-improving life made possible by a whole society of people seeking to be moral.

Morality cannot exist without free trade, without the freedom that gives people the opportunity to produce their own happiness and to enjoy their own lives. Morality is not about giving things away or paying taxes; it is about creating value and keeping that value, it is about living without fear of government. Morality is not about guilt; it is about enjoyment and pride. That makes you a good person, not Bernie Sander's re-distributionist "values".

The altruism card is an attack on your happiness. When dealt to you, it does not make your life better. Just look at the state of our economy. Every regulation, every tax dollar taken from you, every massive government program, every unnecessary war, would not have been possible were it not for their using the altruism card.

They have convinced you that sacrifice would mean a better life for everyone. But the altruism card is not about a better life. Sander's morality is about destroying your ability to be moral. It is about destroying your values.

Left Versus Right Versus Right Versus Left

I respectfully disagree with some of my friends regarding moral equivalency between the left and the right today. Both groups have evolved over the last few decades in different directions that give the lie to they idea that they are morally equivalent. The left has moved toward dictatorship while the right has split into several groups, some of which are not so good either.

The left is now advocating oppressive government as a solution for virtually every fabricated emergency they can divine. Some on the right have gone in the direction of free markets and individual rights. Others still want to ban abortion (a violation of the individual rights of women) and advocate a Christian theocracy. Both groups, with the exception of the small group advocating laissez faire, are replete with pragmatism which leads to corporatism, corporate welfare, government regulations and compromising with the social agenda of the left.

I am not here arguing that you become a Republican. I *am* advocating individual rights and a "hands-off" approach to dealing with citizens. In my view, the laissez faire approach of radicals for capitalism is the correct approach and this calls for a complete separation of this small group from the others on the left and the right. This view holds that the government should be limited to protecting individual rights and prohibited from violating them. I am also advocating that we re-establish a Republican form of government with checks and balances and separation of powers. I am advocating a

Bill of Rights similar to that established by the Founders. The only things I would change with the Bill of Rights is the eventual elimination of the IRS (and the income tax) and a new amendment which prohibits government from interfering in economic transactions and business practices.

We are no longer in a political situation in which the left seeks to extend the American dream through small incremental "changes". Today, the left is a mad dog. They are inventing crimes, engaging in Nixon-like dirty tricks and doing everything they can to disenfranchise the right by nefarious means. In fact, they abhor capitalism and successful individuals. We are fast approaching a time when the rich are considered evil with death in store for them. That would not be new for the worldwide leftist movement.

It is not difficult to conclude that the left wants to create an elite group of "takers" who will re-distribute the wealth of the rich. The takers are made up of people who have no problem confiscating the properties of individuals. Nothing stops them from drawing up regulations or edicts that force people to do their bidding. Their idea of enlightened government is best exemplified by the issuance of arbitrary commands that must be followed - or else. Although they pander to ignorance if it benefits them, they have no regard whatsoever for private individuals whose taxes must pay for their grand ideas and cronyism.

In fact, the left is made up of criminal cabals whose goals are to use government to force through Congress various "business deals" that launder money back to their politicians, judges and criminal gangs. For instance, as part of this cabal, one individual (among many partners) could be working in a high-level position for the FBI refusing to investigate a corrupt company and tomorrow working a high level board position with the same company. Protected by a cabinet official, and protecting that cabinet official, all he has to do is what he is told. This is criminal gangsterism.

These shifts of focus for both left and right have brought us to a critical point as a nation. When so much is on the line, someone must take a stand for freedom. That stand must be held without compromise. This requires opposing "legal" theft by government. This requires the understanding that there is no moral equivalency between a thief and an honest person or between collectivism and freedom. Anyone who seeks compromise is working for his own destruction. You cannot have a little bit of total sacrifice; just as you cannot chose to be a little bit moral. As Dr. Tara Smith observes, "If individuals *owe* one another their services, they can be licensed no freedom to shirk that obligation."[3]

Because collectivism and altruism are immoral ideas, it is imperative that we be uncompromising when defending

---

[3] Moral Rights and Political Freedom, Dr. Tara Smith, Rowman and Littlefield Publishers, Inc. Page 78

their opposite principles (freedom and individualism). As individuals, we must block collectivists (of the left and the right) from using government to advance their goals.

Yet, our current form of capitalism is not a true capitalism. Ours is an injured system because of moral compromise, mixed premises that enable coercion and the willingness of some people to live with or countenance evil. Organizations like the Business Roundtable are made up of CEOs who seek to feed at the government trough, eager to play at free enterprise while they secretly seek to sell the government the rope that will be used to hang them. When working with government is tantamount to preaching freedom, corporate pragmatists are selling out on the principles of free enterprise and economic liberty. We cannot compromise on freedom and live.

Collectivism and altruism like that found in the Business Roundtable mean the sacrifice of some for the sake of the group. They mean enslavement, imprisonment and the destruction of man's mind. They demand conformity and submission. Collectivists will not rest until they have destroyed the best among us. We cannot allow their victory.

We don't need to get along with the radical left; we need an open fight with them (a political debate about principles) and we must win that fight with better, more rational and more practical ideas. If they resort to force, we can only answer them by openly resisting; and we must give them their just deserts. We cannot act like they are our moral equivalents. We must fight them at every turn, and we must convince people that the best way to have a good life is to live free of government coercion.

27

Defending American Values

"The virtue involved in helping those one loves is not 'selflessness' or 'sacrifice', but integrity." - Ayn Rand, Atlas Shrugged

This chapter is an open letter to America's military troops, firefighters, emergency responders and police officers. As a military veteran, I've had a strong interest in military matters since I left the Army in 1968. Even though I considered the violation of my individual rights to be wrong (I was drafted into the Army), I still felt that I was involved in a struggle for freedom for myself and those I loved. During this time, I saw the Soviet Union and Communist China as clear threats to our liberties, and I was convinced that only the United States had the power and ability to stop the advance of totalitarianism. Because of this, I undertook my service with the same patriotic attitude as anyone who had voluntarily joined the military. I believed that our country was still worth fighting for; that it represented freedom around the world against two encroaching tyrannical enemies.

Many service members distinguish themselves by their willingness to sacrifice for others. They take seriously the idea that a moral life is one spent in service to others. They agree with Einstein that

"Only a life lived for others is a life worthwhile."[4]

---

[4] Interview, 1932, The Journal of Young Israel – also New York Times

But I dissent from this view. Today, as a much older and experienced veteran, I challenge the concept of duty that is being taught to members of our protective services. I'm convinced there is a better concept that enables them to express their benevolent natures. I don't think that the decision to protect Americans is a sacrifice.

Most young people today are unaware of the ideology surrounding the concept of duty and its negative aspects. They see themselves as practical people who understand how to protect, and they see sacrifice as an effective way to create good outcomes. Yet, although they have spent their student years listening to teachers and theologians who support sacrifice, they have not been taught about the contradictions implicit in the act.

The first contradiction is that sacrifice is an obligation, not a freely chosen option. According to this view, there is no choice about sacrificing. The second contradiction is that sacrifice should be total; one must sacrifice all of one's time and money for others. As Dr. Tara Smith has observed, "If individuals owe one another their services, they can be licensed no freedom to shirk that obligation."[5]

These contradictions imply some important questions about altruism's role in society. Many take it to be benign and even beneficial. Yet, Dr. Smith asks: "If the paramount altruist objective is to serve others, what is

---

[5] Moral Rights and Political Freedom, Dr. Tara Smith, Paperback, Rowman Littlefield Publishers, Inc. Page 78

the need for freedom? Its role is hardly obvious. Why shouldn't the altruist simply seek to install rulers who will dictate peoples' activities, seize their output, and reroute the proceeds to those in need?"[6]

Indeed, history's most brutal periods were those in which that premise of altruistic sacrifice dominated. According to this view, government officials are authorized to decide men's actions for them and people with guns will be responsible for making it happen. This means that the instrument for implementing sacrifice on behalf of the government will be soldiers and police officers. These professionals will be responsible for coercing citizens rather than protecting them. Is that proper in the land of the free?

Few service-members are aware of the exploitative nature of the moral philosophy known as altruism, the philosophy behind the injunction to sacrifice. Neither have they realized that our nation was the first to liberate people to pursue happiness, *not* sacrifice. So, for service members, the questions are "If Americans should be free to live in freedom, why should you be the instrument of forcing them to sacrifice?" and "How can a protector of freedom and self-interest be required to sacrifice his life and/or limbs while doing his job?" Isn't it a contradiction that he should be forced to give up his life so they can live in freedom and luxury?

---

[6] Ibid

Let's see if we can understand this contradiction more fully.

When the United States was created, a new idea, an anti-sacrifice idea, challenged centuries of moral thought. When the Continental Army fought against the British, our soldiers did not see their American Revolution as a sacrifice; they saw it as a struggle for their own freedom. They did not want to live under a tyrannical king, and they knew that they had to put their lives on the line; they had to fight and possibly die so they could be free. They knew that a tyrant demands nothing less than the lives of those who disagree with his policies. The American Revolution was a matter of life or death for every revolutionary, soldier or citizen.

As our government was originally conceived, and because of the legacy of the Declaration of Independence, a professional soldier in the Armed Forces was different from any similar soldier of any other country. This is because he was a protector of free people, not a protector of slaves. It was not his job to coerce citizens and make them do things they would not otherwise do. His job was to facilitate and protect the citizens' freedoms.

The concept of duty, on the other hand, is centuries older than the concept of freedom. It derives from prehistoric notions in which men were required to give their best children (or their own lives) to appease the gods of primitive religions. Eventually, human sacrifice became so onerous that men wanted, instead, to give up something of lesser value, their best cattle and/or agricultural products rather than their children. Down to today, this idea of sacrificing for others has lost many of its bloody roots and has evolved into a more benign form of "moral action" ostensibly engaged merely to help others. But even this form of altruism, as with all forms in the past, is still seen as a sacred duty to be performed because society or God demands it.

Even as history moved forward, and as altruism evolved, men were sometimes required to give their lives for various social purposes such as war. At other times, they may have been required to sacrifice their first crops of the year, or goats and other animals. However, the distinguishing characteristic of all forms of sacrifice was the obligation that the individual give up a higher value for a lower. Each sacrifice, whether it was a goat or money, meant additional work for the sacrificer so that he could make up for the loss.

The best way to understand what a sacrifice consists of is to compare it with a mutual trade. You do business with the grocer because he makes available products that provide nourishment to you. The grocer charges you what it costs him to buy the product and he adds a markup which is his profit. You are willing to pay the markup because otherwise, you'd have to spend your own time growing or making the product. The benefit to you includes the benefits of consuming the product as well as the time saved in making the product yourself. This is called a mutually beneficial and voluntary trade. Both parties gain; you save time and effort and the grocer makes a profit that enables him to survive and keep providing products for sale. If you take his profit away from him, you remove the incentive for him since he would not be able to feed his own family. That profit is his paycheck.

If you persist in your demand that the grocer not make a profit, you have given him no choice but to use his produce to feed himself only. He will no longer sell it to you; which means your demand that he sacrifice his profit has led to your starvation. The next step is force and slavery. You hold a spear to his throat and demand that he produce the products that will feed you. You tell the grocer that it is his duty to serve you and that there is no choice about it.

Now, imagine a different situation in which government forces you to pay more than the average profit for this product. Let's assume that the grocer is given a monopoly by government and that you are forced by buy your groceries from him at double the price. This would be a sacrifice on your part; in this case, you are required to give up more of your money than you would in a free trade and you are prohibited from making or growing the product yourself. You'll also have to work twice as many hours to earn the money to buy the product and you cannot spend that money on a less expensive alternative. You ask the government what are they doing with the exorbitant profit they are making by controlling the price of the product and they tell you they are giving free health care to poor people. You shut up because you know that is a good thing. What you don't know is that government officials are also stealing much of that money to buy expensive homes and yachts for themselves.

Every sacrifice of this type is an immoral imposition on you. It requires that you act in a certain way and that you lose a value that is more important to you than what you were gaining at the previous price. It assumes that the tribe or state is the repository of morality and that it can decide what you can gain or lose. It assumes you are the property of the state and your purpose in life is to do as you are told. This is altruism in practice. Who is getting the double price that you have paid? – The government, of course – a party that has not earned it.

As Harry Binswanger has pointed out:

"Average Americans naively take the morality of altruism to mean good will, generosity, and human decency. But stripped of that benign cover, the operative doctrine is that your life is not your own, that selfless service to the needs of others is the only justification for your existence."[7]

According to this scheme, there is no such thing as a sovereign individual; the individual is a mere citizen whose purpose is to advance the will of the leaders. These citizens will be fed a lie about a society where all citizens

____

[7] http://www.forbes.com/sites/harrybinswanger/2012/09/10/obama-hears-your-whining-and-hes-here-to-help-you-out/2/

work together but this is mere propaganda designed to convince people that they are not being forced; that they are complying with the government willingly in order to create a better world. This better world is a pipe dream; it will never happen by these means.

Throughout history, few have challenged the idea that sacrifice is moral. They challenged only what made up a proper sacrifice and who should be made to sacrifice. They never questioned altruism. Yet, if we take a dispassionate look at the idea of sacrifice, we must ask, is the original reason for sacrificing, to placate the gods, a valid reason for sacrificing today? Was it even valid in the past? Haven't we, as civilized people, moved past the ancient arguments for pre-defined and obligatory moral action? Further, is the modern reason for sacrifice, the idea of helping others, a powerful enough reason to invalidate the choices and decisions of individuals? Ayn Rand would tell us:

"It stands to reason that where there's sacrifice, there's someone collecting the sacrificial offerings. Where there's service, there is someone being served. The man who speaks to you of sacrifice is speaking of slaves and masters, and intends to be the master."[8]

With the Declaration of Independence and the American Revolution, people fought, not to be sacrificial victims, but to be free. They realized that they had the ability to decide for themselves without the interdiction of a king

---

[8] Ayn Rand, The Fountainhead

or ruler. They could trade freely and build up their property while working free of expropriation by government. This new idea was based upon the real-life experiences of Americans living in the wilderness who knew that their lives could only be successful when they took freely chosen actions. They were rugged, independent and they guarded their liberties diligently. They saw any encroachment as morally reprehensible and they developed, without knowing the monumental import of it, a new morality for living on earth.

Dr. Tara Smith has made an excellent argument for the fact that the call to sacrifice and the concept of individual rights are incompatible:

"...it is vital to respect freedom (including the freedom to do wrong) because a person can only do the right thing if *she* chooses right action. Freedom is a necessary condition for morally right action. Without freedom, individuals would have no chance to act morally..."[9]

"...my claim is rooted in a more basic conception of the nature of morally proper action. An action does not become right until it is chosen and performed by a free person. That choice is part of what makes an action right."[10]

Surprisingly, none of the major advocates of sacrifice throughout history have offered a reasoned argument for

---

[9] Moral Rights and Political Freedom, Dr. Tara Smith, Paperback, Rowman Littlefield Publishers, Inc. Page 78
[10] Ibid

why sacrifice is good. Neither Jesus, Plato, Augustine, Aquinas, Hume, Kant, Comte, Marx; not even Pelosi or Bernie Sanders has offered an argument for WHY sacrifice is good. They have merely relied upon an assumption that it is good. Some have said that God says so, that you will go to heaven, that society demands it and that it is practical but there has never been a tangible argument for why altruism is anything other than the giving up of a higher value for a lower one.

In fact, the strongest (and still false) argument for altruism is determinism, that the individual is imperfect, that he does not have the ability to decide for himself; that he is evil by nature and that he can only be made good by being forced to do what is right; forced to give up something he values for the sake of society.

Determinism is not the philosophy of the Enlightenment; it is the opposite of the idea that man has volition and can determine his own actions and achieve his own happiness. Determinism invalidates the human mind and makes individual human choices into immoral acts, into mindless revolts against God or society. It is an ancient and hateful view of man that justifies enslavement and dictatorship. If you believe that man is a determined creature bound to sacrifice, then you have no problem if millions of men are slaughtered because they had the "impudence" to have been born. If men are determined and doomed by fate, the death of one or a million men is irrelevant.

In fact, altruism has been disproven by the enormous success of the United States that was built on a different moral mandate. Haven't we seen the validity of freedom and capitalism in the very lives we live? Isn't our clean, paved, strongly built and infrastructure-reliant society better than the dirt, hovels and shanty towns of other countries dominated by determinism and altruism? Isn't the reason for our success that we enable self-interest and choice, that people can chose to live clean, happy and self-confident lives?

When we look to the period of the founding of our society, we see that the enlightened view of man held that it was wrong to force men to do anything against their wills, that men had wills of their own and that they were not determined by any historical or universal premise. The United States effectively outlawed the various forms of sacrifice that had devastated societies of the past. In fact, this new form of society protected men in their pursuit of values. It did not expropriate their belongings or demand that men give up things for the sake of others. And this is where you, the defender of freedom come in.

This new society even developed a new form of loyalty. Men were no longer required to be the dutiful slaves of kings or dictators. And because freedom made people more prosperous, they realized, as a matter of self-interest, that this society was worth defending from attack. They created a new concept of patriotism based upon love for a country that valued and protected self-sufficiency and individual rights. This freedom created the concept of American exceptionalism. We were right for reality and that made us better people who deserved to be protected and defended against the plundering dictators and politicians of the left.

The beginning of the end for freedom started during the USA's first decades when Europe exported the ideas of Immanuel Kant. Kant made an assault upon reason (in the name of reason) and free will (in the name of free will). For Kant, because man had the ability to deny his own self-interest, duty was considered a "categorical imperative"; unquestionable and built into the very concept of morality itself. I won't go into all the arguments made by Kant except to say that his philosophy is a massive fraud based upon unproven assertions and deceptions whose result was the institution of irrationality and, once again, force against the individual. America had barely begun to build its economic power before someone tried to kill it.

Of all the evil arguments made for sacrifice, the evilest was Kant's. He claimed that duty was to be done without reward, without a love for man, without even the happiness of heaven as a reward; but simply because it was, in his mind, a duty. This philosophy was a prescription for nihilism and destruction. Enter the destroyers, Hitler, Stalin, Mao and many others who declared that dissent was a crime and mass murder was a solution. Each murderer murdered millions in defense of altruism, sacrifice. None of them offered freedom and affluence; they only offered suffering and death – in the name of duty. What they gave mankind was monstrous evil – and still Bernie Sanders admires them.

At base, Kant asserted that "pure reason" (an idea that he concocted with leads from Plato) had to be totally disconnected from reality; that it consisted only of tautologies. This perpetuated and amplified many of Plato's mistakes and left the human mind incapable of reason. The ultimate expressions of Kant's views resulted in men who could not resist the call to sacrifice and became the fodder for the killing fields, the concentration camps and the mass graves that punished those who refused to sacrifice for the collective.

Certainly, you are going to say that Kant's idea of sacrifice and the murder of millions is not what you think of when you think of altruism. But, whether you realize it or not, that is what altruism means and intends. The idea of human sacrifice has always meant that the best people should be forced to give up their highest values, their minds and even their lives, for the sake of others. The 147 million people killed in Soviet Russia, Communist China and Nazi Germany were the best people in those societies; capitalists, small business owners, intellectuals, college professors, college-educated citizens; people who disagreed (on one issue or another) with their government. They died because sacrifice was considered to be a moral imperative and those who did not agree with it had to be removed so history could move forward toward a world of sacrifice.

The idea that sacrifice is the justification for murder seems incongruous today considering the positive view most Americans have of the idea. Today, many people mistakenly think that hard work for the sake of reaching an important goal is sacrifice. Politicians will tell you, when they are giving their resumes, about all the sacrificing they have done, as if their willingness to sacrifice makes them worthy of votes. Others will downplay or even hide their success because they are afraid to be thought of as selfish and not worthy of votes. These are all examples of the influence of the idea that it is moral to sacrifice.

Yet, the idea that sacrifice is good includes the idea that not sacrificing is evil. This is the basic reason that people do so much to advertise their past sacrificial actions. These actions are like tickets to humanity, verification that someone is a good citizen (according to altruism). Were it not for the demand that people sacrifice, people would not feel so uncomfortable about exerting their self-interest. Even Plato insisted that society should force men to sacrifice for the good of the whole.

I say this is all wrong. A willingness to sacrifice does not warrant deep respect and votes. In fact, a desire to succeed and enjoy life requires much more in terms of hard work and dedication. It requires individual effort, thought, education, reasoning ability and a desire to succeed. The hard work you do today to accomplish a high value or goal is not a sacrifice. Hard work is the price one must willingly pay in order to accomplish a supreme goal. Hard work can only be a sacrifice if it is demanded of men by moral or physical force. If a value did not require hard work and supreme effort, it would not be a high value.

As Craig Biddle writes, "Altruism is not about moral obligation as such; it is about a specific kind of moral obligation. Altruism does not call for a person to serve others if he has made an agreement or a commitment to do so—as in the case of a doctor who contracts to provide a patient with medical care in exchange for payment, or an employer who contracts to pay an employee in exchange for his work. Such obligations are chosen obligations, obligations stemming from mutually beneficial agreements, agreements in which both parties gain a life-serving value. Altruism is not about chosen obligations. It is about "unchosen" obligations or "duties."[11]

And this takes us back to you, the person whose job is to protect. If you are voluntarily fighting for freedom, it is because you value freedom so highly that you are willing to risk physical damage or death. It is a chosen obligation that you take on as a free individual. Therefore, you, the protector of American lives, are being highly moral and pursuing your highest values when you must go to war. You are not sacrificing. You are protecting the right of people to be free and moral. And since you are a human being seeking to live a moral life, you are fighting for your own freedom above all.

---

[11]   http://www.theobjectivestandard.com/issues/2009-fall/creed-of-sacrifice-vs-land-of-liberty.asp

Anyone who tells you that sacrifice should animate your life is doing a disservice to you and to the principles which guided the Founding Fathers in creating this country. They ignore the basic reason why people live in a free society. They ignore the requirements of human survival and they don't understand that freedom leads to happiness. You are not fighting for sacrifice, you are fighting for the possibility of happiness for every American including yourself.

How do people survive in this world? Certainly, they have to identify their true needs and find ways to meet them. But before this, they have to do something much more profound; they have to conclude that life is worth living; that it presents the individual with an opportunity for enjoyment and good living. In other words, people must choose to pursue values which lead to happiness and success. Then, they have to think about how to pursue those values. They realize they have to be productive, do good works and earn the money necessary to survive; they have to engage in a process of reason.

If life did not have the possibility of happiness, there would be little incentive to produce and trade with others. Like the grocer forced to sacrifice his profits in our earlier example, there would be little incentive to develop technologies that lighten work and enable more production. In fact, without the possibility of happiness, it is unlikely that people would want to pay other people to protect them and their property. There would be little need for an army, a police force, firefighters or even society. And this gives us an important clue to why so many societies fail and live in squalor. Squalor is the nihilist's dream. Nihilists must destroy all values and that is what altruism brings; the destruction of values. Who would fight for that? Who would produce for that and who would create values in such a society?

Since men must use reason in order to survive, this brings up the need for people to respect each other's rights to engage in reason, to produce and keep the results of their work. To steal or legally expropriate production would restrict and make impossible the thought and work necessary to survive. Property rights are the first step in creating civilization. By respecting the property of other citizens, we make it possible for people to thrive and flourish. As Ayn Rand wrote,

"Civilization is the process of setting man free from men."[12]

With all this said, I would like to propose an American approach to doing your job of protecting Americans and their property. I think you should consider yourself a professional who honors your own life and that of others. Your chosen profession to protect people is a means for accomplishing your values and goals; your love of life and your love of freedom. Since freedom makes a good life possible for Americans, why not be a protector of freedom paid by those who have hired you to do it? This makes your career a means for engaging in trade with other citizens rather than a mere sacrifice. Further, it

---

[12] The Fountainhead by Ayn Rand

eliminates the performance of your job as a duty and turns it into the performance of your job as a life-serving career. It also eliminates your acquiescence to the false idea that society has a right to demand your sacrifice or that your job is about forcing people against their wills.

To clarify this, ask "What value do I provide when I do my job?" Certainly, the answer must be that you protect individuals, their freedom to live and their properties. In an advanced society such as ours, someone should provide such services and be paid for it. You save peoples' lives, their properties, their freedoms; and your presence in society is a high value. You help people live profitable lives so you should also profit from the performance of your job. It is honorable to earn a profit.

Now, let's imagine that you have a great ambition to be successful. If the level of service you provide is higher than that provided by others, then you should be able to demand a higher price for your services or attain to a leadership position and receive higher pay. Certainly, you must keep your prices competitive, but if you want to earn more business, you will need to add value to your services. You might undergo advanced training, or take additional classes in self-defense, or find the best new technologies, more advanced weapons or surveillance equipment. You may even add new services to your capabilities that are difficult for your competitors to duplicate.

You may also want to remove as much danger as possible from the performance of your job. You may want to use bullet proof vests or other safety equipment. These would make you safer and enable you to plan a long life, get married, have children and plan for their futures. Because of your expertise, you may even be able to invent new tools or technologies to help protect you and your customers. By making yourself more efficient, you increase your chances of survival. You secure your long-term happiness; you honor your values, perform work you like, help people secure their lives and improve society.

As you can see, altruism is the opposite of self-interest. Altruism leads to dictatorship while self-interest requires political freedom. Altruism demands that men be forced to sacrifice. Freedom enables independent thought, free will, capitalism and human survival. Given these facts, what is the proper perspective on doing your job?

Military

The job of the military in the United States is to protect the country against attack by foreign invaders who seek to enslave the citizens. It is not the job of the military to accomplish social goals such as building roads and bridges unless they are needed to help win wars and end conflicts. It is also not the job of the military to force citizens to act against their wills. As an agency of protection, the military should be called upon only when the nation or its interests and possessions have been attacked. As a defensive agency, the military is not responsible for the deaths and rights violations that are the collateral damage for the enemy in war. A free nation places the blame for these deaths squarely on the party that engages in aggression. The US military makes it a point to exact retribution from all aggressors and their agents.

The solder is not a sacrificial tool for the social goals of his leaders. Your time and training should be focused on making you into the best and most lethal fighter in the world so no other country would dare attack us. A good military strategy prepares the country so well for war that the cost of attacking America will be visited upon our enemies many times over. Your job should be to kill the enemy and do it fast, so the war is over quickly, and the enemy is removed as a threat. Then you go home.

Further, your job is to protect the Constitution of the United States. This document has given you a special mission unlike any mission of any soldier from any other country. Our nation is the first nation (and still only one of the few) that is based upon freedom. In defending the Constitution, you are defending the freedom of Americans to live their lives as they decide.

Even today, almost every American "service-person" loves his life; and he knows that only a free person can truly enjoy it. By extension, he also understands the importance of freedom for every individual in society. Perhaps, he even understands that freedom, as Dr. Smith states it, "...is necessary for moral action."[13] The soldier may not agree with everything free people do in their

---

[13] Moral Rights and Political Freedom, Dr. Tara Smith, Rowman and Littlefield Publishers, Inc. Page 78

lives, but he knows that freedom makes it possible for a rational person to live and enjoy his or her life. As a lover of life, an American soldier is uniquely situated to be a defender of the highest values.

Finally, as an indication of the immorality that is created by altruism, many military people are required to sacrifice their lives by utterly irrational rules of engagement. When a soldier must refuse to defend himself for the sake of "non-combatants", he is not only needlessly putting his own life in danger, but he is also allowing the enemy to escape and fight another day. These rules of engagement politicize the fighting of wars and destroy the military's ability to fight and/or win wars. Other issues, such as using the military to build civilian infrastructure and to create talking points for political elections, tarnish the military and its mission.

Police Officer and FBI

The same principles described above apply equally to police officers and others who fight crime. Like members of the military, police officers are equally special because of their dedication to values and their willingness to put their lives on the line to protect people. The difference for a police officer is that he must interact both with law-abiding citizens and law breakers. This gives him a different relationship with the Constitution because he must know the difference between peaceful citizens and those who violate their rights. He must also recognize his responsibility to maintain the Constitution by upholding the rights of all citizens and maintaining high standards of integrity in the performance of his duty.

For instance, a police officer cannot violate a citizen's right to privacy. He cannot insist that citizens keep silent about any issue, he cannot come into their homes without a warrant and he cannot arrest or detain someone without probable cause that a crime has been committed. He can neither harass citizens, threaten them nor defame them. He must treat them with respect and maintain the principle that a citizen is innocent until proven guilty. These rules place a special burden on crime fighters and ensure that they are protectors of rights and not violators of them.

Firefighter and other Emergency Services

Firefighters and emergency services providers save lives and property from fires and other emergencies and have a special connection to the community. At any moment, they may be called upon to have a direct impact on the lives of family, friends and other citizens. When the emergency services professional is not saving lives and homes, he is often training to stay in shape or improve skills.

Although the connection to the Constitution is further away for these individuals, they are equally committed to the values of America and her communities. They value life and operate within the auspices of society in a way that seeks continuity, safety and security, all of which are values derived from freedom. By preserving property and life, they contribute to the values of America.

Generally speaking, military personnel, police officers, firefighters and other emergency response professionals have a strong love of life and they feel a strong sense of satisfaction in knowing their careers help people live better, healthier and more secure lives. It is not surprising that some of the best people choose these rewarding and fulfilling careers.

I believe that having concern for others is not a bad thing and it need not involve the sacrifice of higher values for lower. It is a natural extension of the idea that you love life, that you honor it and that you respect the freedoms and uniqueness of every human being. Freedom, self-sufficiency, love of life and family are valid American values that are worth protecting not only because you want to enjoy them in your own life but because you see them as an extension of the greatest idea in history, the United States of America.

Thank you

"Whatever your holistic plan (socialism or fascism) is, there are some people who will never fit in. This includes those who do not share your vision of a better world and never will. They will have to be neutralized somehow." – Lester Hunt (parenthesis mine)[14]

The above statement exposes an ominous state of affairs as we move closer to a more domineering government. Mr. Hunt, in criticizing totalitarianism, is also criticizing the progressive movement that is somewhat hindered from achieving its goals by the U. S. Constitution. Like typical totalitarians, they would prefer not to be hampered by limited powers.

Yet, as totalitarianism advances, and as the constitution is chipped away, the left's methods for dealing with dissent move slowly from propaganda and historical revisionism toward more drastic methods such as imprisonment and summary execution. It does not matter the society, once a government attains full power, it must do what it thinks it must do. The Germans during the Nazi period were considered to be among the most intelligent and educated of societies, yet they descended into barbarism and a lust for murder.[15] There is every reason to expect that our leaders will descend to these depths as well. Given their ideological fervor and the belief that they are right, one

---

[14]   http://lesterhhunt.blogspot.com/2009/11/nazism-or-communism-which-is-more-evil.html

[15] See The Ominous Parallels by Dr. Leonard Peikoff

should expect that they will deal with dissent in much the same way the Nazis and Soviets did. Especially when you consider some of the worrisome things they have done such as asking citizens to report their neighbors to the White House.

We have not arrived at summary executions yet. However, the left's strategy for neutralizing opposition deserves scrutiny. The left's minions are doing everything possible to stay in power if the FISA IG Report is any indication. An article called "The Self-Made Man is a Right Wing Myth" by Tim McGowan of the Philadelphia Progressive Examiner is an example of how progressives use ridicule to manipulate dissent.

"Let a Democrat say we need to raise taxes on the wealthiest 1% of the population and his call will be met with howls of protest from the Right saying that is punishing success. They portray taxes as Socialist wealth redistribution, an onerous and unfair burden, and confiscation. They then defer to a story of the self-made man a la John Galt in Ayn Rand's Atlas Shrugged as the model of how they succeeded and no one gave them anything and the poor deserve to be poor because they are lazy losers. We are the winners by dint of our superior ability."[16]

---

[16] http://www.examiner.com/progressive-in-philadelphia/the-self-made-man-a-right-wing-myth#ixzz1nQ77DoFO

This caricature of what the "Right Wing" would say to a call for more taxes is itself a myth. There is little evidence that today's wealthiest 1% are working "a la John Galt", the brilliant fictional character who stood firm against collectivism by going on strike.

Unfortunately, most of today's self-made men are not intransigent defenders of their own rights. In fact, most of them agree with the idea that men should sacrifice for the sake of the "common good". Regarding their superior ability, they might point to a good education, gained through a private college, most often paid for by working part-time jobs and surviving lots of sleepless nights. They became successful by unrelenting hard work, clear thinking and dedication to a purpose, but they are also cowed by statements like those made by McGowan. In fact, they tend to blame themselves for the failures of others. They think, instead: "We didn't train our employees well enough to do their jobs or we failed to inspire the spirit of accomplishment in them".

Yet, the point of making a caricature out of successful people is to denigrate anyone who would complain about the government's massive debt. Additionally, the left wants to "head off" any of the stronger arguments about the value of the individual in society. They accomplish this by defining their enemies as something they are not so they can easily dispose of their arguments. They'd prefer to preemptively ridicule any statements that men make against the advance of statism. The government realizes that those who truly understand individualism, capitalism and property rights must be neutralized; and the easiest way to do that is to ridicule them before they raise their heads to complain. It helps that they control the media and the message.

Mr. McGowan continues:

"Many a millionaire will laugh and explain to you that the self-made man is pure fantasy and is largely based in someone's ego, arrogance, insecurity and ignorance, as well as just plain old fashioned fiction cooked up by frauds like Grover Norquist to give justification to an essentially selfish, greedy, and destructive economics that benefits virtually no one but 1% of America's population."[17]

This paragraph provides us with a clue to the essence of the argument against capitalism and self-interest. Contrary to Mr. McGowan's denials, his statements are indeed intended to punish success by means of several anti-concepts such as "arrogant, insecure and ignorant" that he uses to describe successful people. The purpose here is to turn positive traits into negatives. The positive traits that actually describe most successful people are "work hard, dedicated, desirous of a better life and studiously intelligent". But these traits, the correct ones, don't serve the purpose of the looters. So self-made men must be diminished and punished while their true motives are ignored. Theirs is the method of tyrants.

I consider name calling of the self-made man to be undignified, mean and hypocritical. But the key issue

---

[17] Ibid

here is the tactic of ignoring the positive traits of successful people which sometimes results in a feeling of invisibility and worthlessness within the self-made man. It is the same tactic once used against slaves who were supposed to consider themselves useless if the "master" disapproved of their rebellious nature. It is easier for a tyrant to control the man by controlling the mind.

The true value of those individuals who bring us computers, communications systems, iPhones, electricity and automobiles, not to mention thousands of other products and services, should be acknowledged and appreciated not ignored. Not only is it illogical for Mr. McGowan to play these "mind games" with today's self-made men, he barely strives for accuracy. He assumes that everyone knows what these words mean and that everyone agrees his ridicule is justly earned. I think it is time to challenge the left about its punishment of success. It exposes them as hypocrites and manipulators. A true "man" knows his own measure and he doesn't need a pretentious non-man to tell him his value.

For instance, why is it evil for a person to seek his own self-interest (to be an egoist) but good for a person to be poor? If the egoist is trading value for value in pursuit of his self-interest, why is that evil? The same goes for such concepts as "selfish" and "greedy". What do these terms mean in actual practice? Is the act of being honest in one's dealings, making good products and services and trading those products for reasonable compensation selfish or greedy? A man of pride would say, "You're damn right. What of it and why does it mean so much to you?"

To answer these questions, we must understand that in order for the left to continue looting American society, it must eliminate the possibility of self-made men. It wants them to continue to be productive, but it does not want them to think they are vital in any way. Further, in order for the left to establish the framework for slavery, it must destroy the idea of inalienable rights. The best way to do this is to denigrate those who would benefit most from the protection of fundamental rights, those people willing to work the hardest for success. If such people can be "educated" to consider themselves unimportant then what the government takes from them is also of little value.

Notice that progressives love to praise themselves as being dedicated to helping people. They give themselves awards for helping the downtrodden, the poor, the ignorant and the sick, all the while ignoring the fact that they do these things with the money created by the self-made man. They take credit for supposedly helping millions of people when they have not spent a single dollar of their own money. They glorify themselves, write books about their lives, erect statues of themselves and name buildings after themselves while ignoring the real accomplishments and success of the very people who make their massive government programs possible. For progressives, the real achievement is that they took somebody else's money.

Yet, the short-term "pragmatic" goal of progressives like Tim McGowan is to neutralize the opposition from accomplished individuals who want to defend their rights, property and incomes from government expropriation. This explains the use of such terms as "John Galt" and "self-made men" in Mr. McGowan's article. These are terms straight out of Ayn Rand's writings and the left is running scared to stop her influence.

Of course, progressives don't call what they are doing "looting" or "slavery". They prefer to say that we live in a grand collective where all men, as long as they work hard for others, can create a fair society. They rhapsodize about a "social contract" where some are asked to do more because, according to them, society has given them so much. We receive a "social safety net", great schools, health and human services and so much more from society. They praise the state for providing us with streets and highways to transport the rich man's products. For progressives, this means that each humble contribution from the individual is a gift from each to all. If such a sacrifice is not willingly given, then the unwilling must be "neutralized". Those who disagree with giving their "fair share" and playing by "fair rules" must be shamed for harming society. You really didn't build that, leftist do-gooder technocrats made you rich. Now genuflect and worship the state.

Progressives ignore the fact that government does not ask, it commands; and any government that commands does not have to worry about whether citizens approve.

For instance, many government workers, because they don't have to compete for their jobs, are arrogant, rude and sometimes "ignorant". Money taken from the private sector will most often be squandered and wasted, and few people will be held accountable for these losses. Those wonderful roads are often full of potholes, the schools teach children the party line and other agencies of government do more to squash trade than increase it. Massive government debt has meant fewer jobs, higher prices, less disposable income, less saving and more poverty. Who pays for the losses? Why the greedy self-made man, of course. As one economist put it, if you spend other peoples' money, cost and quality mean nothing.

But Mr. McGowan springs another more vicious trick on the self-made man. It goes like this: He is not really self-made. According to this view, the so-called self-made man is created by society. Each of us is a product of our environment. If a person achieves riches, those riches are provided by those who purchase from him. We are a collective where all value comes, not from the individual, but from the group that reared and nurtured us.

According to this view, society has first call on anything the individual makes. There are no rights except those that society decides to create. And if society requires that the individual give up something for the sake of the whole, it is completely right to make the demand. Everything the individual receives is a gift from society anyway, and everything he makes originated in society. The group is everything, the individual is nothing.

This view, of course, is collectivism, the idea that the collective is more important than the individual. Its political expression is democracy and its final destination is dictatorship. Collectivism is advocated by people who view society as god. Their ancestors philosophically are Plato, Descartes, Hume, Kant and Dewey to name a few. The goal of these philosophers was to ensure that individuals stay firmly below society (the group) in importance. The result is that the individual never discovers he has rights. If he accepts the notion that everything should be shared equally, regardless of individual effort, then he cannot question the government's effort to re-distribute his income.

Collectivism creates a gross ignorance of several important facts. First, it ignores the individual's role in his own survival. In order to survive, an individual must think and act correctly. How he thinks is his choice. In order to think, he must develop knowledge that is usable, and he must make a choice to use that knowledge. This leads to the recognition that the most important thing about the individual is that he survives by means of reason. Thinking, using reason, is a singular act chosen by each individual, not by society for the individual. Because collectivism ignores these facts, it creates a gross prejudice against the individual and builds a society around exploitation, control and violation of rights. The many gross violations of individual rights create a society of incompetence and poverty.

From an economic perspective, collectivism destroys the results of the human mind by outlawing capital accumulation, savings. Since collectivism expropriates savings, individuals do not have the ability to create abundance. The result is that people stay at the level of mere subsistence. This is why collectivist societies always fail: they must exploit individuals and this very exploitation destroys progress. Once collectivists see their ideas failing, instead of desisting, they blame individuals who are "cheating" and not giving their fair share. These individuals are the most talented in society because they produce more than those who have already been beaten down. The result is more government-approved anti-individualism to fight the government-approved anti-individualism that created the decline in the first place.

We can continue with this line of thinking until we descend further into absurdity. We see that absurdity around us every day, especially in the writings of men like Mr. McGowan. What most people miss is that collectivism creates the very poverty that progressives blame on self-made men. And, the failures leftists want to correct are the very failures their excessive spending has created. In our society, higher taxes on the rich, costly and unnecessary regulations, executive decrees, deficit spending and inflation, as well as the health care bill, have negative impact on the lives of people. They make it more difficult for people to survive and then they blame people for deliberately sabotaging their efforts. This leads to oppressive behavior on the part of government.

Don't think this approach of the left will cease with the biggest collectivist program ever proposed. It is called the Green New Deal and one thing you can be sure of: the New Deal will be a Big Steal.

In order to understand the basis of Mr. McGowan's arguments, we must understand the way collectivism and democracy work. Progressives have long advocated collectivism and democracy for the simple reason that politically, these ideas enable them to gin up votes and outrage among the poor for collective action. That collective action must always require sacrifice for the sake of the collective. The poor, of course, will not be doing the sacrificing so they'll vote for it. Collectivism and democracy are not about love of mankind; they are the methods of gangsterism and theft.

In contrast, a republican society would not allow people to vote away the rights and property of other citizens. In a republic, people could vote for politicians, but they could not vote for the elimination of individual rights. Such a system protects the individual because it recognizes that the only way to have a peaceful, cooperative society is to ban force in human relationships. Individuals, free to secure their survival without the threat of expropriation, enslavement or democratic vote, have only cooperation and reason as their means to success. People keep their possessions out of right not out of dispensation from an authority; and this makes possible capital accumulation, investment, improving products and infrastructure not to mention reason and mutual trade to mutual benefit. Property becomes the hallmark of success.

To illustrate the importance of the principle of individual rights, ask yourself what would happen if men could not keep their earnings? This would mean they could not accumulate capital for investment in grand schemes such as a power grid that covered large areas of the country. The result would be people living without electricity. You would also not have large automotive companies which would mean people could not travel for work or pleasure. They would not have telephones, computers, television sets, even food. Without capital accumulation, even if these items were invented, each would require so much human energy to produce that prices would be too high for the average person. Only those with political power and lots of other peoples' money could afford them.

Democracy represents the most corrupt use of force possible in society. Throughout history, democracy has devolved into gangsterism and protection rackets. For progressives, it is the means to an end which is totalitarian control. Once people begin voting away the rights of individuals, democracy becomes tyrannical government. All one gang has to do is claim to be the defender of the downtrodden and it can get away with anything including murder of its opponents. All they have to do is create an emergency, rig a vote and then take over. And today, with the Green New Deal, the re-distributive "democracy" of the left plans on stealing money on an unprecedented scale. If you wonder what the outcome of this re-distribution will be, read the previous paragraph again.

In contrast, our original republican system of government prohibited the government from violating individual rights. The founders of our nation foresaw all of the corrupt ways of doing government, especially the flaws of monarchy and Greek-style democracy. They found a way to eliminate the corruption of these systems through such devices as limited government, separation of powers, checks and balances and the Bill of Rights. They declared that man was free to pursue happiness (which means he could accumulate capital) and their system put up roadblocks against money expropriation.

Since the advent of progressivism (the Wilson years), gangsters have been working to undermine the Constitution and individual rights. Their work is almost complete. We've virtually lost sight of the genius of republican government and of how many problems it solved for civilization. We are moving headlong into democracy, gangsterism and tyranny because we've lost the knowledge that Republican government defends individual rights.

Contrary to Mr. McGowan's words, collectivist government is not the source of the great benefits of society. Those benefits come from those among us who have the ability to think clearly and act. They come from men of genius who bring us the new, the unheard of, the unanticipated and the brilliant. They also come from efficient businesses that make life-enhancing products, distribute them and collect the revenues. Only liberty can create this success; not government interference in the affairs of men, not collective thinking, not sacrifice. Success cannot happen without human energy, dedication, long hours of work and the desire to make it happen, all of which come from an individual decision, not from society. This fuzzy idea that the greatest men of capitalist achievement owe their success to society is poppy cock. Where was such individual achievement before the capitalist era that liberated human intelligence?

To prove my point, I challenge government to take the laziest welfare drunk from the dregs of society and turn him into a millionaire without giving him a handout. Come on, if successful people owe their success to society, then who is going to be the first liberal to start creating millionaires? This argument that millionaires are not self-made is nothing more than an excuse for robbery. We are turning into a nation of cannibals.

But Mr. McGowan did not write what he did in a vacuum. This kind of charge against self-made people is very common. It happens thousands of times a day in our country. Punishment of success is deemed proper by many people. In fact, some people take such criticisms of self-made men as morally unanswerable. Why?

Why are people like Mr. McGowan allowed to get away with hatred of success? Why do people give his criticisms such credence? Why do so many men accept ridicule for the mere act of trying to live? I think the reason is that throughout the centuries men have been brainwashed to blame themselves whenever something goes wrong. It seems to be a natural tendency to accept blame for things over which men have no control.

Add to this the influence of many philosophic systems that start with the premise that man is imperfect. This view is derived from ancient myths in which men did not heed the demands of the gods. In response, the gods punished men for their apparent arrogance and demanded that men pay retribution in the form of sacrifice. Early men were taught they had done something dis-respectful to the gods and deserved the fire, earthquake and other storms that were dispensed. Since then men have accepted the idea that they deserve to be punished even for their success. The result was centuries of societies barely capable of supporting themselves because of stultifying ritual, tradition and much sacrificing.

Once religion won out over reason in ancient Greece, there was no historical standard bearer for reason. Religion began a steady growth and men began to look inward to solve their problems, to pray, to humble themselves, to blindly accept blame for presumed vanity, arrogance and selfishness. Those rational men that were still left became silent, and in order to stay alive they submitted to the cruelties and insults of religious leaders and kings. Monarchy became the tyranny of the period and anyone who challenged the king and/or god was certain to die, be tortured on the rack or ridiculed in front of the entire community. Men knew they had better keep their heads down lest they lose them for the sake of heaven's wrath. The result was the Dark Ages when seeking knowledge was a sin and disease and hunger were common.

I think it is accurate to say that these collectivist influences have given men an inferiority complex of sorts. They create a tendency among men to blame themselves whenever other people are said to be suffering. They are taught that greed is evil merely because they want to acquire assets. They are taught that they have excessive pride merely because they want to do well. They are taught that their success takes away from the success of others and they do not question the veracity of these teachings.

Psychologists will tell us that the best way to cure neurosis is for the individual to connect with his past, to go back to those situations where his thinking went wrong, relive the negative experiences and correct the flawed thinking. Yet, most psychologists don't know how to help people bring out their rational and more assertive possibilities. They countenance men to "be yourself", spontaneous and whimsical. They tell men adjust to social forces and try to get along, unaware that they are not curing anyone; they are not addressing the dominant philosophical teachings that cause men to be troubled.

What these people have missed throughout the centuries is that man, by his nature, is an autonomous being with the capacity to understand, to reason and to decide for himself. Man can be successful in nature and in society; but it is important that society not punish his success. It must protect the rights of men to succeed and enjoy life.

This idea of protecting individual rights became possible for the first time during the Enlightenment when men realized that life could be an adventure, that the individual could determine his own course and that independence from authority was the key to successful cognition. At this point in history, men began to "self-create", to educate themselves and to develop the personal character traits that enabled them to explore, to invent and to produce. These new character traits brought about the rise of men who understood how important freedom was to successful living.

Contrary to what Mr. McGowan might say, these men made a difference. The Founders were men of action and of independent thought. By setting the intellectual foundations of America in freedom and man's free will, they made possible the success of other men such as Thomas Edison, Henry Ford, Andrew Carnegie and many more who invented huge enterprises run by new principles of efficiency that benefited men tremendously. The whole character of the society was poised to liberate even more men, to increase their independence, their mobility, their intelligence and their vision of the future. At first, government did not regulate this; it merely protected men against criminals and politicians.

It is often said that in the American system, the rich get richer and the poor get poorer. This is said to be a flaw in the system that makes it exploitative and unfair. The opposite is true. Consider that in America a man could invest his capital to create huge industries that benefited millions of people. Let's say a given individual creates a grid for the production and transportation of electricity over broad areas. This grid made possible immeasurable improvements in the lives of his customers. What did he get for his investment? His customers gave him mere pennies in return for comfort, more productive living and the lighting and heating of their homes. Who became rich in this scheme? The real benefit went to the customers. All the industrialist received was money.

Contrary to Mr. McGowan's cynicism, individuals do matter and they do make a difference. Any success they create is theirs to appreciate and enjoy. And the more they create the more credit they earn, the more honored they are and the more appreciated they should be. Men seeking to "actualize" their own potential, once they have done the thinking, the hard work, the long hours and the building of great enterprises, are important and vital to the futures of all men. They make it possible for other men to actualize their potential in ways previously unheard of. Not only should they be appreciated, but they should appreciate themselves, obtain a great sense of pride in their accomplishments, and they should learn to defend and protect what is theirs. They should know they deserve their success.

Statements that punish success such as those of Mr. McGowan are based upon hatred of man and a desire to enslave those whose work they seek to expropriate. As for myself, I see man's purpose to be the ultimate enjoyment of life and I admire men who seek to "make" themselves. I want to be like them rather than envious of them.

To counter Mr. McGowan, I suggest that egoism is not evil. Arrogance is often the proper response to people like Mr. McGowan who mindlessly criticize what they don't understand. Insecurity and ignorance characterize the critics of self-made men; they are not characteristics *of* self-made men. Selfishness is not evil but the normal character trait for any human being whose purpose is to survive. Greed is a meaningless concept based upon a negative view of success and accomplishment. And destructive economics is actually the province of progressives who would denigrate men's characters and steal their wealth.

But the real problem is more than just an inferiority complex imposed upon the vast majority of men. The real problem that creates men like Mr. McGowan is the philosophy of altruism. He would not be able to get away with his cruelty without the dominance of a philosophy that demands sacrifice as a moral imperative. Only altruism combines a pretended love of mankind with the expression of hate for the successful.

Only altruism can demand that successful men pay ransom to those who are not responsible for their success. Only altruism justifies murderous hatred and makes the mere desire to live into a crime.

The fact that men like McGowan (and their readers) accept altruism is why they get away with ridiculing and insulting independent Americans. Altruism gives them a mandate to pretend to be morally superior. Someone should expose their illogical assumption. Where would they be if someone pulled the altruism rug out from under them and exposed altruism for the barbaric and murderous idea that it is? More than likely, they'd be on the streets begging for a handout.

Without altruism and its acceptance, self-made men would be free to create a magnificent future based in freedom and pride.

Changing the Debate

"No man ever prospered by unjust practices, but in a righteous cause there is hope of safety." - Euripides 480-406 BC

The tactics, goals and methods employed by the Obama administration; the bailouts, the stimulus packages, the executive orders and the unilateral rules-making, including a host of trial balloons to re-distribute income, failed with the American people and the left was voted out.

Yet after three years of Republican control, we are headed into gridlock which may not be a bad thing. Many Democrats said to Republicans don't go after this program or that; right now is not the time to go after NPR or the Affordable Care Act; we have more important issues to address; getting people back to work and improving the economy.

Some people say we should keep our hands off of programs that represent a gargantuan amount of theft. This debate within a debate to keep the welfare state intact threatens our ability to act at all. It sends us into impeachment of the President as a way of protecting the welfare state and the grip of the Democrats on our money.

The strategy behind this obfuscation is due to the desire of Republicans and Democrats to hold on to their control of our minds. Both sides want to continue the spending banquet regardless of how much damage is done to the lives of real people. They don't want change, despite high deficits, so they avoid meaningful reform while promising reform every election cycle. They are the problem.

A different, though not new, idea came out of the Tea Party revolution of 2009 and 2010. The idea that the Constitution meant something important emerged. This was a hopeful sign that was unfortunately stillborn. So, I'd like to offer my suggestions for defending American values in an effort to give a voice to people who would like to restore them.

I think the Bill of Rights expressed one principle that will help us understand what the Founders had in mind. The principle of individual rights holds that each individual is a sovereign agent who has a right to make his own decisions about life. I use the word "sovereign" to contrast individual rights with the idea of sovereignty of the King or of the government. When we say that the individual is sovereign, we negate the idea that anyone else is above him or in control of his life. No one, neither King nor government has the authority to dictate the choices that the individual is responsible for making on his own behalf. This precludes any government regulation that would tell an individual or business how to operate, the decisions that individuals may make in the marketplace when selecting products and the moral choices they might make when it comes to their most important decisions when dealing with others in society. It assumes that man is capable of deciding for himself and that his mind is competent to affect his survival. It also assumes that man is able to use reason to decide for himself as well convince other individuals to cooperate and trade with him. In other words, by right, according to the nature of man and of how he survives on this earth, no one has the authority to dictate to him what he will do. The only constraint on the individual under this premise is that he or she must also respect the individual rights of others.

The principle of individual rights means no income taxes, no welfare, no income or power of re-distribution of any type and especially no interference in the individual's personal choices about what he will buy, what he will sell, what he will say, with whom he will associate, what he will think or believe, what he will do with his money and property.

Yes, I said it. No income taxes. If anyone wants to contribute to the functioning of the government, such contributions should be voluntary or on a pay as you go basis. Use taxes are not out of the question if they cover costs without markup. There may be other non-coercive ways to fund the government. For instance, a gofundme account can be set up so citizens can contribute to the specific government "services" they believe in.

I would like to make it clear that I am consistent in my advocacy of individual rights. These rights belong to all individuals including women who have the individual right to control their futures and their bodies. No one should be forced to do anything against their will, and they should not be prohibited from making decisions about their health and futures.

Once the principle of individual rights is established, we must agree not to look for exceptions or find arguments that justify violating these rights in delimited ways or in any way. This first principle, the principle of individual rights, is inviolable and the individual who is thus liberated, as long as he does not violate the rights of others, must then live with, suffer from or prosper as a result of his individual choices. Even charity must be a freely chosen act.

Because we know that reason is the singular most efficient faculty possessed by man, and since we know that once left to their own devices, most men will seek to live according to the best exercise of their minds, we know that the result of a society based on individual rights, the best possible outcome, will be a vast realm of peace and prosperity.

As I wrote in a past blog post, "Do You Know Your Rights":

"You have a right to make a living. This means you can create your own job by learning skills and selecting the profession you desire. More than this, you have a right to be proud of making a living. You should never accept the idea that you owe something to a collective or to others. The idea of having a moral obligation to "give back" to society is a collectivist notion intended to make you feel guilty and exploit your production for the sake of despots. The more freedom you have to make a living, the better society becomes. Likewise, the more the government creates jobs paid for by the money of other citizens, the worse our society is becoming. You do not have a right to a job created by government for the purpose of giving you an income.

"You have a right to what you create. If you use your mind to create a product, that product is yours to trade with others or to keep. Your production cannot be taken from you for the sake of a collective that thinks it knows what to do with your work. In order to be productive, you had to use your mind and, because of this, whatever you produce is yours by right. You also have a right to be proud of what you create. You should never accept the idea that all production and creative thought is a collective endeavor undertaken for the sake of the group.

"You have a right to make as much money as you can possibly make. You create wealth by producing and if you have invested time in educating yourself, spent money in buying the tools of production and worked hard for hour upon hour, the money you make, all of it, should be yours to keep. No one, especially the government, has a right to take it.

"You have a right to say what you think without fear of disapproval from others. Your mind is your property. It is an expression of your excellence and of your ability to ascertain reality. Just as you respect the right of others to think, your right to think should be respected as well.

Only when you are free to express what you think are you living in a society that is just and fair. If government assumes the power to tell you how to think and how to express yourself, you are living in a society that considers you a slave. If government attempts to punish you for your ideas, you are living in a dictatorship.

"You have a right to be moral. Whether you are young and inexperienced or old and wise, you are the decision maker about what is right for you. No one has the authority to dictate to you what you should do. As long as your actions do not violate the rights of others, you have the ability and the obligation to decide for yourself what is moral.

"You have a right to your own philosophy. Whether you accept a religion or a secular philosophy or decide upon your own philosophical views, no one has the right to tell you how you should think. Just as in any other decision, if you accept wrong ideas you will have to deal with the consequences. No one can force you to accept a given religion or body of ideas at the point of a gun or by law.

"You have a right to associate with whomever you like. This right is an extension of the fact that you have a right to decide what is moral. No one has a right to demand that you go to group meetings, that you repeat slogans and that you think group thoughts. You are a free person and you can do as you please so long as you do not violate the rights of others.

"You have a right to all the energy you can use…there is no way you will ever use more energy than is available to the planet. The more energy you use, the more you can produce and the more money you can make. As long as your energy use does not harm the property or lives of others, you should use all the energy you can to make a better life. Anyone who says you are harming the planet is trying to destroy your mind and stifle your ability to enjoy your life.

"You have a right to privacy. What you do in the privacy of your own home is your business so long as you violate no other person's rights. No one has a right to invade your privacy without due process of law whether it is a policeman or a census taker. You have a right to your body and your health. Your health decisions are yours to make in consultation with your doctor. The government can never tell you what to do with your body. You have a right to choose your doctor, choose your treatment, choose your method of payment and no one can violate your body and tell you or your doctor what to do.

"You have a right to protect yourself against violence and fraud. The government that seeks to prohibit your right to self-defense is a government intent on robbing you. You have a right to live where you want. As long as you are able to trade income for a residence, you are free to live where you choose. No one can tell you what house or what neighborhood should be your abode.

"You have a right to trial by a jury of your peers. A fair trial using objective laws and logical argument is the only way you can keep thieves and government from destroying your rights or stealing your property. It is also the best way to fairly settle disputes among citizens in civil cases.

"You have a right to capital accumulation. Capital accumulation is the method that enables you to grow your wealth. Savings, astutely invested, should never be skimmed by government. When the government assumes the right to take your savings by means of money inflation or direct taxation, it is operating as a thief. You have the right to keep your savings in whatever form you see fit such as gold, silver or secured paper. The government has no right to decide for you what currency you should use.

"You have a right to make your own economic decisions. The government has no right to intervene in your economic matters, business operations, banking decisions, transactions or more. It does not have the right to tax your property away or tell you how you should act economically. It has no business regulating your business and as long as you are not defrauding anyone, it should always be "hands off" of your economic activity.

"Each of these rights is an extension of the concept of individual rights. If our society respects these rights, then we can have a vibrant, healthy society, diverse in people and in opinions, where the best ideas win and where there is no limit to how far you can advance. It is a secure society because there are no threats to the individual, where people can trust one another and where self-sufficiency and respect are the hallmarks. Let no one tell you that freedom is the gateway to sin or that self-interest is evil. Never let them tell you that freedom has failed, and it is time for central planning. The man who tells you that is a thief. Freedom is the gateway to accomplishment, to cooperation, to reason and to happiness. Anything else is slavery."

If our elected leaders would keep these principles in mind and recognize that the government does not have a justification, nor does it have a prerogative to violate these rights, we'll know our priorities going forward.

In addition, we should look closely, not only at the 16th Amendment, but also at the Interstate Commerce provisions as well as the "general welfare" clause in the Constitution and interpret them, properly as restrictions on government action, not as license to act. There is no valid justification for the violation of individual rights by government – which means that the common interpretations of these clauses are invalid. Any effort to use them to justify government coercion must be opposed and stopped by the people.

The principle of individual rights is the principle that can guide our politicians as they move forward. The only proper "social" goal of government is to respect and protect the rights of individuals.

This is the debate we should be having.

Ugly Unwashed Savages

We've seen it before: the moral outrage aimed at America in places that still don't have running water. Our children may be too young to know, but those in my generation also saw this outrage on television when we were young - from places all over the world, ginned up by pro-Soviet agitators who railed against capitalism and the evils it had supposedly done in the world. Most of these people are now wearing American blue jeans and riding their bikes to real capitalist jobs so they can feed their brood.

But the arguments of the America haters are the same as they were in the past, America is evil, America is imperialistic, America robs the poor and leaves them destitute. Forget that these are lies; today's protesters are repeating the same line...without the help of the KGB. Even the flag-burnings and effigy-burnings are the same. Hate America. Destroy America.

In difficult times throughout our past, Americans have been exceptional. Where others have been hateful and bigoted toward us, Americans seek reason, understanding and fairness. Where others have gone into the streets and expressed hatred for our way of life, we have been (too) tolerant and respectful of their views. When many of these people are devastated by disaster, our nation is the most generous in providing aid. In spite of our goodness, our media has striven to show hateful images of angry faces of foreign protestors hating us because they want us to think we should accommodate them in some way. By this reasoning, we are evil, and they are right to hate us. Today, our leaders insist that we should not respond to these endless provocations so that the savages won't have a reason to kill us. Elliott Ness where are you? What happened to the idea of fighting evil rather than accommodating it?

I think it is time to send the savages a message. Why do we continue to keep quiet while these poverty-laden idiots on the streets are depicted as morally righteous? Why do they consider us "ugly Americans" intent on dominating the world when we have been the liberators against tyranny of more people than any other nation? Their contorted expressions of bitter hate are not based on anything we have done, but upon lies told to their leaders by our university professors. It is time to realize that if anyone is bigoted and bullying it is not Americans; it is those who pretend to have moral outrage against us. We are the good people in the world, the best that have ever existed, the most civilized, the most educated and the most respectful anywhere. Anyone who has moral outrage against us must be a hater of the good.

Today, as we stand in the shadows of remembrance of the vicious hatred and murder of our fellow citizens, we strive to think deeply and carefully. Despite the fact that many of our leaders agree with the America-haters, many of us are silent. We seldom defend Israel because our leaders no longer support the only real bastion of freedom in the Middle East. We seldom defend our capitalist system when it is the only system that has brought abundance and relieved more poverty than any dictatorship that hates us. We keep hiring American university professors who spout archaic and invalid Marxist lies about capitalism to students from all over the world. If anyone is responsible for terrorism and hatred of America it is American college professors. We seldom defend our right to our abundance and we elect leaders who are bent on giving it away to those who scratch rocks for food because their leaders won't let them be free.

It is time someone told the anti-Americans all over the world what we think of them; they are uncivilized, ignorant, barbaric, poorly educated, bigoted and totally undeserving of the attention they get from our media. We really don't care about their fake anger.

The time for hating America is over. The time for saving freedom has arrived. Don't tread on Americans. We will not submit. We will not relent. You can call us racist, bigoted, hateful and astro turf, and repeat as many other lies as you want. We know what we stand for. Individual rights, without compromise, without silence.

We don't care what those ugly, unwashed savages are told to pretend to think.

On the Fringes of Power

Once again, the Progressives have exposed themselves as unable to lead or govern. After decades of planning, scheming, scandalizing, dividing and lying, they took power in 2006, completed it in 2008 – and are once again back on the mere fringes of power. The American people, according to the left, are still clinging to their guns and religion. So, the left, as it moves forward, will continue to cling to its (government) guns and Marxist religion.

What they don't understand is that they fail because the don't understand that it is in the nature of all socialist states that they are incompetent and inefficient. This is because individuals are better at running their own lives than are government technocrats who think they are smarter than the American people. Yet, the free American is able to learn from his own mistakes while the people trying to rule you don't even know you. When a government official tries to run your life, he constantly interferes and only learns from the most massive of his mistakes. And, when he must change a failed policy, he always says, "I need more power". Remember that when you are thinking of voting for Bernie Sanders or any politician who says he can "fix" something that is not working in society. He always "fixes" *his* so-called problems with your money and freedoms.

Leftist central governments create these government technocrats who make the biggest mistakes that you must pay for. They get a raise and more power to interfere in your life. You get to be a slave. You get to obey and it is you who must feel guilty for the failures caused by leftist governments. They never look into the mirror and ask whether it is their policies which have failed. Instead they insist that you must change, you must become convinced that altruism and collectivism and re-distribution are the solutions – when it is altruism, collectivism and re-distribution that have caused the problems in our nation.

It is leftist Democrats who must look in the mirror. If they did this, they might realize they need an actual agenda FOR America if they are to win. But they are too invested in buying votes through re-distribution and Trump has now taken that away from them. And the Green New Deal isn't selling. The people know the Democrats can't run such a massive program. The failed Iowa App proved that. They have nothing left but what they started with: hate and force. Hatred of capitalism and violent revolution for the sake of a lost cause.

Have the progressives learned a lesson? Have they reviewed the flaws in their thinking, corrected the mistaken premises that caused their electoral defeat? No, they are continuing with their strategy of feigned superiority based on feigned outrage at demons they have created. Below is a list of the strategies they will employ going forward.

1. As long as we allow them to participate in the debate about governmental policies, they will offer us an incrementalist strategy. They will give us a mix of

solutions, some good, most bad, from which to choose. Through this process, they hope that we will compromise with them and allow them to continue their advance toward more coercive, more rights-violating re-distribution schemes.

2. The left will continue with their divide and conquer strategy by attacking the fictitious "Military Industrial Complex", our troops, as well as our past wars and military actions. The goal here is to denigrate our power in the world and our ability to defend freedom against dictatorship. Their criticisms are designed to prejudice the American public against the fine soldiers in the military as well as the justified actions taken on behalf of freedom and the long-term stability of the world; and especially our desire for a peaceful world. By turning the tables, so to speak, making *us* into the dictators and murderers of the world, they undermine our strength and willingness to defend ourselves; and this destroys the freedoms acknowledged in the Constitution and our need to fight for them when necessary.

The left claims that their goal is to fight war mongering and special interests that need war in order to make profits; but what they want to attack is the profit motive itself, the idea that a free country can produce abundance and become a bulwark against the thieving dictators that the left has turned into victims. They want to diminish the value of capitalism which improves lives and requires security and defense by our military. If they can destroy our industries, they can make us weak and destroy our freedoms.

3. They will continue to divide us by means of the various groups that they contend exist in our country. They will designate certain groups as victims and others as oppressors. These divisions are myriad and ever-changing based upon which divisions yield the most immediate political gains at any given moment (To understand this more fully, read my book "Crushing the Alinsky Radicals"). They will pit black against white, Hispanic against white, rich against poor, rich against middle class, middle class against indigent, Hispanic against black, Muslim against Christian, Arab against Jew ad infinitum because each of these divisions add up to a sum which equals decline of American values.

The problem for the left, with this approach, is that Americans generally dislike being corralled into groups, and even new immigrants will seek to individualize themselves and strive for affluence. Oftentimes, by the time the left has created a major ethnic or racial division politically, the people in the designated groups will have moved on into the middle- and upper- middle classes through their own diligence and hard work.

4. Once again they will debate among themselves about how they are going to mainstream socialism. This has always been difficult for them because people generally reject the notion that it is their duty to sacrifice their hard-earned income for the sake of others, especially if it is accomplished by force of law. People work hard enough as it is, and they don't like being forced to work harder for the sake of others who do not earn their own keep. There is a sense of injustice about it. The left will

always debate about the difficulty of having to present themselves and their socialist views to the voting public. Giving the voters a choice in the matter always means electoral defeat; so they will do everything they can to create scandals and crimes to disenfranchise their political enemies. Don't be surprised if they also seek to steal elections and create massive numbers of fictional voters and voting blocks.

In fact, after a major electoral defeat, when the idea of re-distribution has been rejected, they often delude themselves by crying that if they had only admitted they were socialists they might have been able to "sell" the idea and win a mandate. This "realization" has led them to do just that and, as we write, they are busy offering the most outlandish impossible boondoggles that will give them total control of the economy and lives of citizens. The Green New Deal and the collectivization of their base as well as other programs such as Medicare for All, the various Global Warming schemes, free college education, etc. will require such massive budgets that we'll never get spending under control. This will force the impending collapse of our economy (which they think will keep them in power forever). Add some phony wars and they'll keep you in chains forever.

Other leftists, who consider themselves to be realists, suggest the incremental approach over time so that one day the people will wake up and realize they have a socialist state and everything is fine and working well. I've suggested before that this day will never come. The more they incrementally impose coercive measures into society, the worse things get. So, the electoral defeat comes anyway. This is why socialism is seldom voted into power when it is a clear explicit choice (think McGovern). Most socialist states in history came into power by means of violent revolution and they too ended in economic collapse. Eventually, and we are getting close to it, the left will have to advocate violent revolution because, by then the American public will have gotten tired of their incessant meddling in our lives.

5. Yet, what keeps the left at the table is an ages-old killer. It is an idea that has insidiously destroyed life; an idea that is so unscientific, so backward and barbarous, a killer that hides behind fake benevolence; an idea known as altruism. Altruism is the belief that man's duty is to sacrifice for others regardless of what is in *his* self-interest. Altruism is a war against self-interest and the mind of man; a war against the individual; and by destroying man's right to pursue self-interest, altruism destroys much of the good that man would otherwise bring into the world. Historically, the losses caused by altruism are staggeringly huge and, if measured, would total billions of lives. The imagined damage to be caused by global climate change pales when compared to the loss of life and human energy that can be attributed to altruism's impact on the planet. In fact, the effort to control industry in order to "save" the planet is, actually, a massive effort to institute altruism as the controlling philosophy on our planet – which will destroy our planet because it will destroy all values and cause millions upon millions of deaths.

The Dark Ages are a good example of the influence of altruism. This period was full of famine, starvation, poverty, early death and illiteracy because the leaders convinced the people that their purpose in life was to sacrifice their minds and bodies for God and the state. When people have no prospect of positively affecting their own futures, when they must obey rules established by overbearing leaders; when "rules" demand their willing sacrifice; when they are not allowed to use their minds, when they never learn such concepts as individual rights inherent in their nature, the result is always death and destruction.

The ritual practice of altruism has been with mankind since the first kings discovered a need to control the masses and turn them into herds of obedient cattle. A religious ritual is a re-enactment by men of the lives of the gods. The most common ritual is the suffering savior allegory about the man who *learns*, through his suffering, that he is good only if he sacrifices for others. Altruism, joined with collectivism, creates the compliant "good" citizen; who mindlessly obeys the edicts of Kings and religious leaders.

Today, altruism is taken for granted, almost to the extent that it is invisible. Point to a problem, offer sacrifice as the solution, and you'll decide that someone must starve so someone else may eat. They'll tell you the nation has enemies; so all young men must sacrifice their lives so the kingdom may grow. Who must sacrifice? It is always the better, the most intelligent, the most beautiful, the most productive, the most industrious; it is always the better person who is denigrated, defamed, humiliated and destroyed, not because he is a parasite, but because he is not a parasite. Refuse to sacrifice and you are the enemy of society, the bringer of evil, the selfish brute who would take rather than give. So go the lies of altruism.

Yet, the flaw in this scheme of moral manipulation is that altruism, because it invalidates the human mind, creates only devastation, battlefields running red with blood, concentration camps filled with rotting corpses, nations looted of their wealth and starving children who have no one to take care of them. This is because altruism is not about being a good citizen; it is about letting men in power loot wealth and human energy under the pretext that things will be better "if you'd only give a little." To convince the citizen that he is only giving "a little" they minimize the value of life, of production, of human inventiveness and of self-reliance. If they convince you that *you* are nothing, then everything they take from you must have little value too.

Altruism is at the base of the ideas of the left and of the right today. Our former President once told a would-be plumber that re-distribution helps everybody, as if this were an unquestionable truth. He was oblivious to the fact that re-distribution destroys everybody. He told us that in order to spur economic growth we must devalue the currency, oblivious to the fact that whenever this form of re-distribution has been tried, it plunders and destroys entire nations. His wife told us that "Barack Obama will require you to work. He is going to demand that you shed your cynicism. That you put down your divisions. That you come out of your isolation, that you move out of your comfort zones. That you push yourselves to be better. And that you engage. Barack will never allow you to go back to your lives as usual, uninvolved, uninformed." In other words, things will be better "if you'd only give up your values." She was completely oblivious to the fact that she was talking down to people as if she were a Queen speaking to peasants who wouldn't know what to do without Her. And if you look at our nation once "Barack" took control, things did not get better as a result of the unprecedented re-distribution he enacted. It was altruism that she demanded; self-sacrifice for the sake of the King.

Will the left give up altruism? Will the right? Will they not see that the opposite principle, the principle of individual rights and the pursuit of happiness, the principle that the state has no right to confiscate the property of citizens is the very principle that did away with the Dark Ages and with concentration camps and economic hardship? Will they not examine the lies in their views? Such as the lie that man is a mindless slave who must do what he is told? The lie that man is meaningless and dirty and selfish? The lie that he can only be happy when he gives to others? The lie that reason doesn't work, capitalism doesn't work, freedom doesn't work?

The question becomes then, why allow anyone who preaches altruism into the debate at all? There is no benefit to continuing the march toward dictatorship. There is no benefit to allowing the left to incrementally advance their force-laden solutions. Why don't we demand our freedoms, stand on individual rights and then let the left respond to us? Why compromise when compromise would mean our demise?

One thing you can count on; the left's strategies for power will not change. The idea of power and central planning are too deeply entrenched in their mindset. According to their critique, capitalism is the scourge of history, the enslaver and the exploiter. In spite of the fact that the lives of capitalist workers today are several magnitudes more comfortable than during the 19th Century, the left's view that the workers are exploited by capitalism will persist. At the base of this view, and of every other re-distribution scheme proposed by people on the left and the right is the idea that the individual has a duty to sacrifice for others. You find it everywhere, on the left with Obama and Soros, and on the right with Beck and the neocons. As long as you believe it too, the thieving politicians will always have a seat at the table. Why should they have a seat at the table when all they do is destroy values? Defending American values should have a seat at the table. We must remove ourselves, the fighters for individual rights, from the fringes of power and never give up our American revolution until we take the Bill of Rights seriously.

About Robert Villegas

Robert Villegas is an Arizona Author specializing in fiction, romance, theater, religion, poetry, philosophy and business books. He was born in South Texas (Weslaco) but raised in Indiana. He has spent a lifetime in the business world as a UPS executive and also worked in locations all over the United States and Europe. He is an Army veteran who served in Korea as a telecommunications specialist serving in the 7th Infantry Division in Camp Casey, Korea. He was educated in Indiana and earned a Degree through the University of the State of NY (Albany) via an external degree program. He is divorced with three grown children and three grandchildren. Famous relatives include Mexican anti-hero Dimas DeLeon and guitarist and music producer Johnny Garcia of Weslaco, TX (lead guitarist for Garth Brooks and Trisha Yearwood).

Mr. Villegas has written numerous books which can be found on Amazon.com or ordered through bookstores.

These four books by Robert Villegas comprise some of the business books that he has written. As an executive working for several companies, he was able to develop these methods that will help anyone seeking to excel in the business world. These books are:

How to Be a Great Employee – and a Greater Manager

You cannot be a great manager without first being a great employee. And this is something that requires learning, experience and attitude. The attitude comes from you but the learning and experience you should acquire through diligent study and practice. http://amzn.to/2BqdG2i $3.99 Kindle $8.95 softcover

SWOT Analysis Supercharged

A SWOT Analysis is an objective look at the internal and external elements of your organization that impact your success or lack thereof. If done diligently, you will always have a handle on what you need to do to improve season after season.
http://amzn.to/2BCAWYx $3.99 Kindle $6.95 softcover

The Five-Module Call Center Training System

The Five-Module Call Center Training System is designed to assist the Call Center Team Leader in helping his employees quickly upgrade their skills to an acceptable level. http://amzn.to/2B3Svj1 $3.99 Kindle $5.95 softcover

Website Development Methodology

Effective strategic marketing requires the ability to differentiate the website development organization and its deliverables from those of the competition. http://amzn.to/2DnYMqh $2.99 Kindle $12.95 softcover.

www.robertvillegas.com

The REAL Purpose-Driven Life
After centuries of being told that it is not about you, it is time to set the record straight. You are a unique individual and your goal in life should be to achieve your own happiness.
https://amzn.to/2XyrpPf $3.50 Kindle $7.95 softcover

Values and Purpose Workbook
This book is about you. It's about time. After centuries of being told that nothing is about you, it is time to set the record straight. You are a unique individual and your goal in life should be to achieve your happiness. https://amzn.to/2XwlkTv $3.99 Kindle $8.95 softcover

www.robertvillegas.com

These three books are based upon a new perspective on the life and person of Jesus. Based upon a new theory of the story of Jesus as an invention of the Roman Imperial Cult, these books add significant new evidence for this theory.

Unkilling Jesus

Starting with Atwill's Caesar's Messiah theories, this book explores the following questions. How was the story of Jesus's life written? Who was Paul and what was his role in the creation of Christianity? What was his provenance and did he actually meet the resurrected Christ? Who wrote Revelation and what was the document's purpose? Why was Domitian assassinated? Who was Clement and what was the nature of his relationships with Peter and Josephus? Were the Pseudo-Clementine materials really "pseudo"? Why did Saulus attack Justus? How were the gospels written? http://amzn.to/2itMCo0 $3.99 Kindle $15.95 softcover

Domitian: The Final Messiah

The central goal of this book is to define the specific themes and concepts that make up Domitian's contribution to Christianity – in a sense, we are defining the specific Domitian overlay to the Christian materials originally developed for Titus. http://amzn.to/2yWMSlx $2.99 Kindle $6.95 softcover

Paul's Agon and the Mystification of History

Paul and Jesus are joined in one important way; the way of a miracle. They met on the road to Damascus while Paul supposedly pursued Christians. Jesus, in a sense, told Paul to get with the program and stop persecuting his people. In this incident, the Bible tells us that Jesus is already dead, and resurrected. This book argues otherwise. http://amzn.to/2zSDsuP $5.99 Kindle $19.95 softcover

www.robertvillegas.com

These four books comprise a system that can be used by both patients and counselors who are battling Alcoholism and Addiction. Based upon Mr. Villegas's own system developed during his struggle against alcoholism, this system includes:

Alcoholism and Addiction – A Secular Ten-Step Program

This groundbreaking book offers a secular approach to alcoholism unlike that offered by Alcoholics Anonymous. We recommend that every individual going for alcohol and drug-abuse counseling be given a copy of this book which contains the workbook and the two versions of The World's first drunk. http://amzn.to/2md6R9w $3.45 Kindle $11.95 softcover

The Secular Ten-Step Program Workbook

This booklet covers the program developed by Mr. Villegas. It is designed as a workbook with blank spaces for the patient to write his own thoughts as he takes each of the ten steps. Order one copy for each patient in counseling. http://amzn.to/2IrHimS $4.49 Kindle $6.95 softcover

The World's First Drunk – With Counselor Talking Points

This booklet is designed for the counselor as he works with patients during individual or group therapy. It contains helpful tips on discussing the life story of the man who invented alcohol. Order one copy for each patient in counseling. http://amzn.to/2I446Wr $2.99 Kindle $5.95 softcover

The World's First Drunk – Patient Version

This version of the short story contains empty spaces where the patient can answer questions about the life story of the man who invented alcohol. Order one copy for each counselor. http://amzn.to/2IdxBGb $2.99 Kindle $5.95 softcover.

www.robertvillegas.com

www.ingramcontent.com/pod-product-compliance
Lightning Source LLC
Chambersburg PA
CBHW070749250726

48662CB00004B/1702